THE SHOT HEARD ROUND THE WORLD

On 28th June 1914 a man named Gavrilo Princip shot dead Archduke Franz Ferdinand, the heir to the Austrian emperor, and his wife Sophie in the city of Sarajevo. This is often seen as the event which started World War One. Nobody then had any idea the war would last for four years and be one of the most terrible in history.

BANG!

THE DOMINO EFFECT

Gavrilo Princip was a Serb who wanted all the Balkan states to be free from the Austrian Empire. Many Serbs felt the same way, so Austria blamed them for the Archduke's murder and declared war on Serbia. Unfortunately this set off a domino effect with all the empires declaring war on each other.

Russia was allied to Serbia and so immediately came to Serbia's aid against Austria . . .

. . . while Germany was Austria's ally and so joined Austria against Russia . . . And Germany had a plan.

GERMANY'S PLAN

For centuries the Germans had felt sandwiched between two old rivals who, they feared, would gang up on them – Russia to the east and France to the west. So they had a plan ready: if they ever got into a war with either one, they'd quickly invade France, who they thought would be easy to beat . . . then concentrate on Russia, who they believed would take longer to get ready for war but ultimately be harder to defeat.

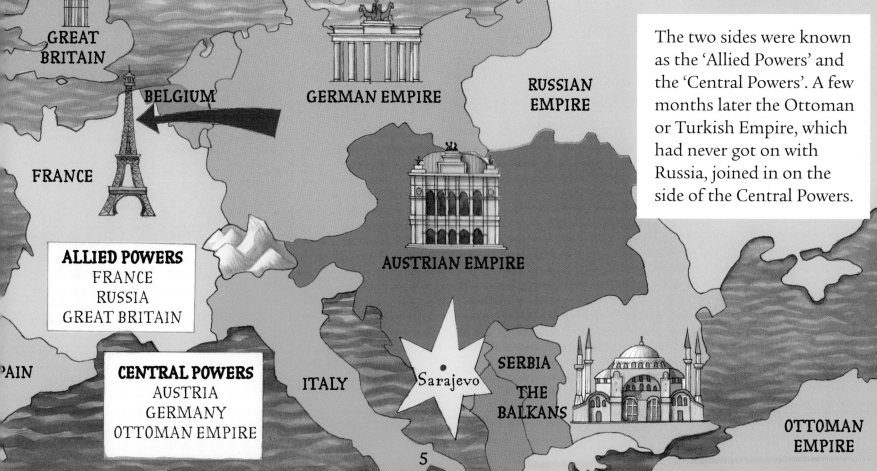

Part of the plan was to surprise the French by invading through Belgium and that's exactly what Germany did. But the Belgians didn't want the Germans marching through their country and asked Britain for help. Britain therefore also declared war on Germany and so, in less than a month, five of the empires were at war on one side or the other.

The two sides were known as the 'Allied Powers' and the 'Central Powers'. A few months later the Ottoman or Turkish Empire, which had never got on with Russia, joined in on the side of the Central Powers.

GREAT BRITAIN

BELGIUM

GERMAN EMPIRE

RUSSIAN EMPIRE

FRANCE

AUSTRIAN EMPIRE

ALLIED POWERS
FRANCE
RUSSIA
GREAT BRITAIN

CENTRAL POWERS
AUSTRIA
GERMANY
OTTOMAN EMPIRE

PAIN

ITALY

Sarajevo

SERBIA
THE BALKANS

OTTOMAN EMPIRE

Crowds gathered in Europe's capitals strangely excited by the idea of war. Huge numbers of men volunteered to fight. Hundreds of thousands of horses were also 'recruited'. Horses had always been used in war for transport and cavalry, but when the French army used Paris motor taxi cabs to rush troops to the Front, it began to dawn on people that machines might soon take their place.

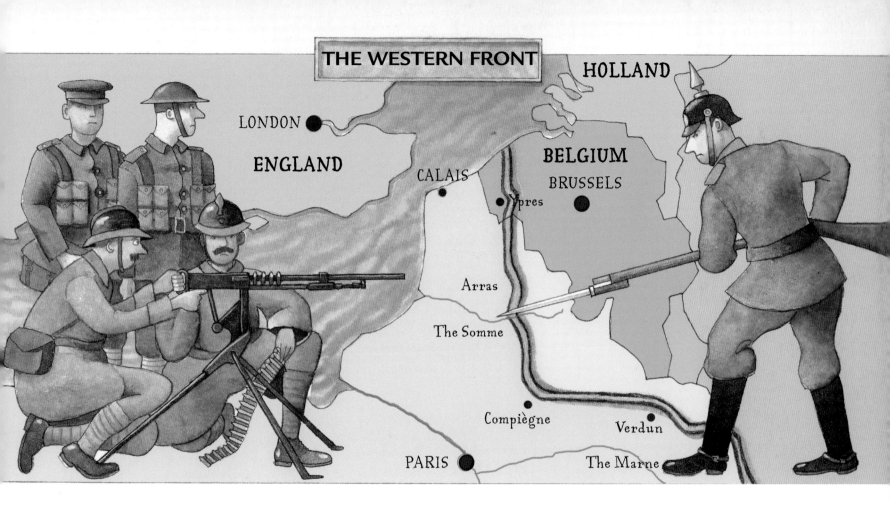

THE WESTERN FRONT

After the German army crossed from Belgium into France the French and British managed to stop their advance. The Germans had no alternative but to withdraw towards the Belgian border. Here they dug themselves in to trenches, with the Allies facing them, on a line that was to change very little for the next four years. This became known as the Western Front. The names of towns and rivers along this line would soon become notorious for the millions who would die there.

World War One was not called a world war for nothing! The European empires had scrambled to grab control of other lands all over the globe, creating their own colonies. Now there were no more left to go around, but the war gave them the chance to try to steal each other's colonies.

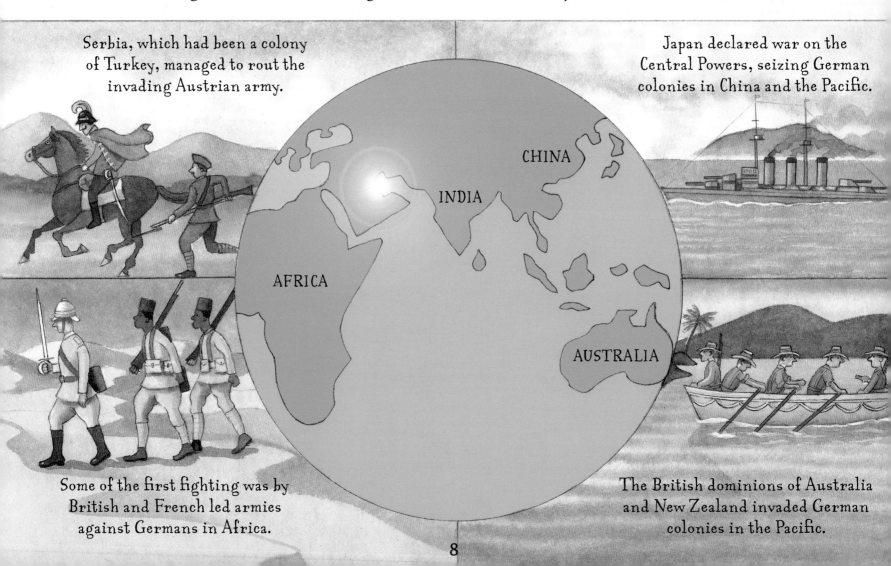

Serbia, which had been a colony of Turkey, managed to rout the invading Austrian army.

Japan declared war on the Central Powers, seizing German colonies in China and the Pacific.

Some of the first fighting was by British and French led armies against Germans in Africa.

The British dominions of Australia and New Zealand invaded German colonies in the Pacific.

CHRISTMAS 1914

Most people had imagined the war would be over by Christmas. When it wasn't, many British and German troops on the Western Front stopped trying to kill each other on Christmas Day. They sang carols and climbed out of their trenches to exchange gifts. Some even played football in the area between the lines known as no man's land. Such acts of friendship would not happen again. There would be too much hatred of the enemy after the slaughter during the following year.

TRENCH WARFARE

Few had expected a war in which machine guns and heavy artillery – the firing of huge missiles, called shells, which exploded when they hit the ground – made it so easy for defenders in trenches to kill attackers crossing open ground. Mostly soldiers huddled in the trenches under constant bombardment. Conditions were appalling.

LATRINES
Toilets were just holes in the ground. They stank.

LATRINES

Pooh!

CONNECTING TRENCH

FRONT TRENCH

Trenches zigzagged, so if a shell exploded shrapnel would not travel straight along the line.

SUPPORT TRENCH

CUBBY HOLE:
Gave a little protection in the front line.

TRENCH FOOT:
Constantly wet feet led to infection. Sometimes feet had to be amputated.

DEEP DUGOUT:
Mainly reserved for officers.

DUCKBOARDS:
To keep feet out of water.

RATS:
Multiplied and grew very large.

Many soldiers remarked on the oddly joyful sound of larks still singing despite the horror and destruction.

NO MAN'S LAND:
The bombardment destroyed every living thing between the lines, leaving only mud and shell holes filled with water. Bodies were left unburied because it was too dangerous to go out and move them.

The spikes on German soldiers' helmets stuck up above the trenches. The Allies used them for target practice until the Germans changed the design.

BARBED WIRE:
Buried deep under the ground. Almost impossible to get through.

GAS:
Both sides used poison gas so soldiers needed gas masks.

MINES:
Tunnels were dug deep under enemy trenches and filled with explosive.

SHELL SHOCK:
The constant shelling left huge numbers of soldiers with trauma - unable to think straight, let alone fight. This was not understood at the time and over three hundred British soldiers were shot for cowardice.

TRENCH COAT:
Designed for British and French officers, this style has been in fashion ever since.

THE HOME FRONT AND THE ROLE OF WOMEN

MUNITIONS WORKERS

POSTWOMEN

LAND ARMY FARM WORKERS

RAILWAY WORKERS

While armies of men shot each other with huge guns at the front, somebody had to make the arms and ammunition. Millions of women worked long hours in munitions factories. In Britain they were known as 'canaries' because their skin turned yellow from the sulphur used in making explosives. This also seriously damaged their health. The work was dangerous. On several occasions the munitions exploded killing hundreds.

NURSES AMBULANCE DRIVERS SUFFRAGETTES

VOTES FOR WOMEN

Millions more women left jobs as servants to do other essential tasks previously only done by men. It would be much harder in future for men to claim women couldn't do men's work and few women were keen to return to being servants after the war. It also made it even more ridiculous that women could not vote in elections. Soon after the war, Austria, Germany, Britain, the USA and several other countries introduced votes for women.

WORLD-WIDE INVOLVEMENT

TIRAILLEUR
FRENCH SENEGAL

BLACK LION
BRITISH INDIA

CHINESE LABOUR CORP
CHINA

In 1915, the Allied powers tried unsuccessfully to invade Turkey at Gallipoli. The force included many troops from Australia and New Zealand, known as Anzacs. Anzacs and Canadians also fought with the Allies in the trenches.

Millions of men from the European colonies left their homes to fight on the Allied side, despite often being treated as second-class citizens. Hundreds of thousands of Chinese were recruited to dig trenches and work in factories. Large numbers lost their lives.

WINSTON CHURCHILL

The Prime Minister who would lead Britain in World War Two started World War One as a government minister. After being blamed for the failure at Gallipoli he went off to fight in the trenches. Later he returned as Minister of Munitions where his support for the development of tanks helped win the war.

LAWRENCE OF ARABIA

The Middle East became another battleground. A British officer, named T. E. Lawrence, was sent to encourage an Arab revolt against the Ottoman Empire. He became famous in Britain as the kind of romantic hero many had imagined before the terrible reality of the trenches dawned.

Countries such as Saudi Arabia, Iraq, Jordan and Syria were only created after the war. The sons of Hussein Bin Ali, who had led the Arab revolt, were each given a kingdom to rule.

WEAPONS AND WAR MACHINES

Many new fighting machines changed the way battles were fought compared to previous wars.

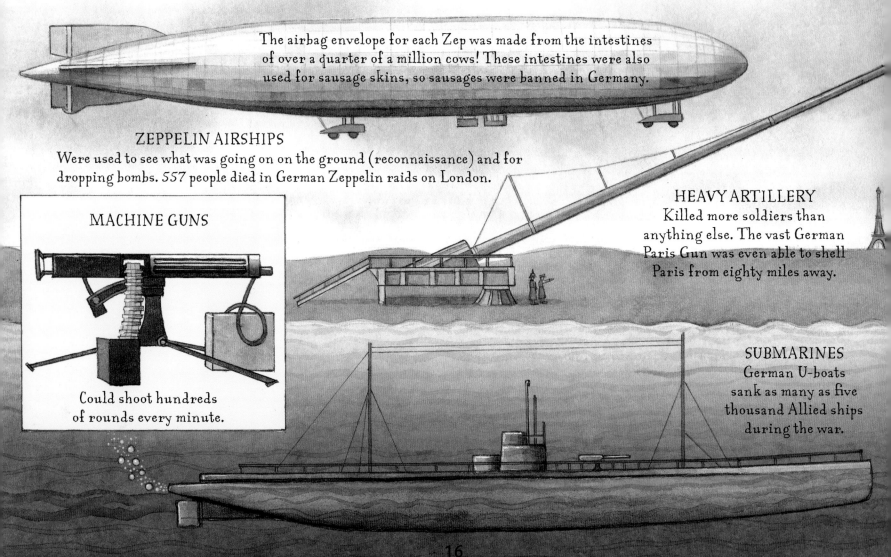

The airbag envelope for each Zep was made from the intestines of over a quarter of a million cows! These intestines were also used for sausage skins, so sausages were banned in Germany.

ZEPPELIN AIRSHIPS
Were used to see what was going on on the ground (reconnaissance) and for dropping bombs. 557 people died in German Zeppelin raids on London.

HEAVY ARTILLERY
Killed more soldiers than anything else. The vast German Paris Gun was even able to shell Paris from eighty miles away.

MACHINE GUNS
Could shoot hundreds of rounds every minute.

SUBMARINES
German U-boats sank as many as five thousand Allied ships during the war.

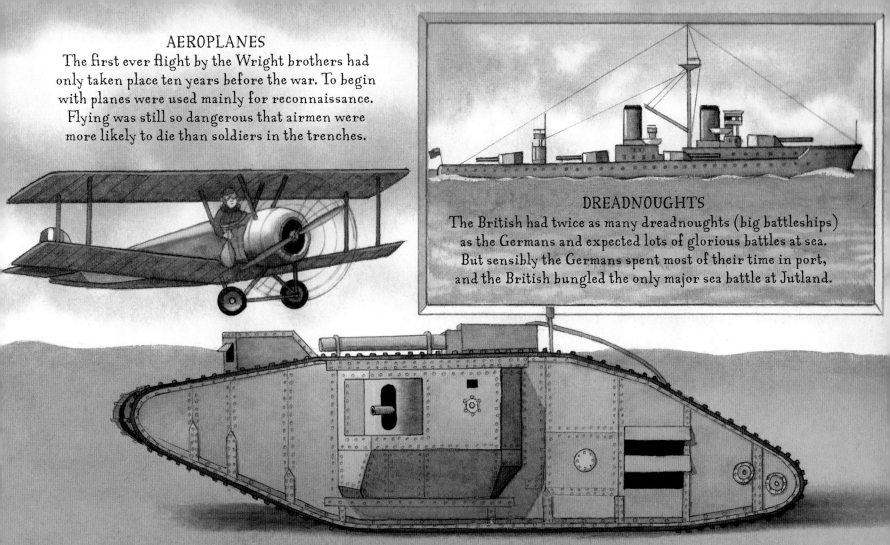

AEROPLANES

The first ever flight by the Wright brothers had only taken place ten years before the war. To begin with planes were used mainly for reconnaissance. Flying was still so dangerous that airmen were more likely to die than soldiers in the trenches.

DREADNOUGHTS

The British had twice as many dreadnoughts (big battleships) as the Germans and expected lots of glorious battles at sea. But sensibly the Germans spent most of their time in port, and the British bungled the only major sea battle at Jutland.

Perhaps the most important weapon of the war was the tank developed by Britain and France. Early tanks were not much good but they got better as the war went on, allowing the Allies to drive over barbed wire and trenches to break through the lines and end the stalemate.

THE SINKING OF THE LUSITANIA

Many people in the USA did not wish to become involved in what they saw as a European war. Opinion began to change after a German U-boat sank the British ocean liner *Lusitania* in 1915 with the loss of over a thousand passengers, including 128 US citizens. When U-boats began deliberately attacking US ships in 1917, America declared war on Germany. The US army was quite small to begin with but the Germans had not bargained for the speed with which they then mobilised additional men.

By early 1918, ten thousand American soldiers were arriving in Europe every day.

18

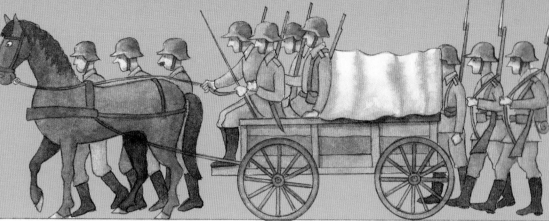

THE RUSSIAN REVOLUTION

By 1917 Germany and Austria had defeated Russia. The Russian armies mutinied and the Tsar abdicated. In March 1918 the Bolshevik revolutionaries seized power in Russia and signed a treaty with Germany.

With Russia out of the war a million German soldiers were released to fight on the Western Front. In spring 1918 they launched one last push which at first broke the Allied line before running out of steam.

After it failed, German soldiers lost heart. Their generals realized they could never find the men or supplies to match those from America. Revolution broke out in Germany. The Kaiser was forced to abdicate and the new government asked for a ceasefire. The Allies agreed, provided the German army retreated back within its own borders.

THE SECOND ARMISTICE

Early on in World War Two, after Germany defeated France, Hitler ordered the same railway carriage to be returned to the same spot near Paris where he dictated to France the terms of an armistice.

The Armistice, which means ceasefire, was signed in a carriage of the Allied commander Marshal Foch's private train. Six months later, five years exactly after Archduke Franz Ferdinand's murder, a treaty was signed at Versailles Palace which officially ended the war. Germany, easily the most powerful of the Central Powers, had to agree they were to blame for starting the war and to pay the cost of the damage suffered by the Allied Powers. By this time Austria and Turkey were so broke that there seemed no point in asking them for anything.

More than sixteen million people were killed during the war. That's more than the whole population of Greater London today. Twenty million were wounded. There were no antibiotics in those days to stop wounds becoming infected and many died or lost limbs as a result. Having all those casualties to deal with led to one of the few good things to come out of the war as doctors found new treatments or developed ways to improve existing ones.

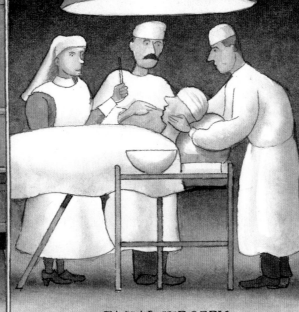

X-RAYS
Marie Curie, the first woman to win a Nobel Prize, equipped twenty mobile X-ray vehicles and introduced radon gas to treat infected wounds.

FACIAL SURGERY
Sir Harold Gillies performed pioneering surgery, rebuilding the noses and jaws of over five thousand soldiers with severe facial injuries.

BLOOD TRANSFUSIONS
The discovery of different blood types and how to store blood led to the rapid development of blood banks for the wounded during the war.

Nearly every European family on both sides lost somebody during the war . . . sons, fathers, husbands, boyfriends, brothers. Many of those who returned were disabled, or had suffered such trauma that they found it hard to adjust to life in peacetime. In an age when women were expected to marry and have children, there were very few young men left to marry.

Only one out of ten of you girls can ever hope to marry. Nearly all the men who might have married you have been killed.

1914-1918

SPANISH FLU

In 1918, as if the war had not been a big enough disaster, a terrible pandemic known as the Spanish Flu spread among soldiers and civilians alike. It killed far more millions than the war itself – as many as the Black Death had in the Middle Ages.

WAR MEMORIALS
You'll find one in almost every town and village. Sometimes the list of those who died includes almost all the young men who left to fight.

HOW THE WAR CHANGED THE WAY PEOPLE THOUGHT ABOUT EQUALITY

Many ordinary soldiers who had fought on equal terms with officers in the trenches returned home determined to have more say in running their countries.

Many soldiers from the colonies who had fought side by side with Europeans returned home determined their countries should have more say in running themselves.

The Great War, as it became known, solved hardly any problems and created many new ones. With the collapse of the German, Austrian, Russian and Ottoman Empires, the Allies drew lines on the map to create new countries. Many people found themselves in countries they did not wish to be part of. The resulting disagreements meant that, only twenty-one years later, there would be a new world war.

ARMISTICE DAY

In 1918 the Armistice came into force at eleven o'clock on the eleventh day of the eleventh month (November). Every year since, those who died in war have been remembered on this day, which is known as Veterans Day in the USA and Remembrance Day in the Commonwealth.

In Flanders fields the poppies blow
Between the crosses, row on row.

Surely this must have been the war to end all wars.

At the burial of a comrade, Canadian John McRae noticed how poppies were the first flowers to grow on the bare earth of soldiers' graves. His poem 'In Flanders Fields' inspired an American, Moina Michael, to wear a poppy on Armistice Day in 1918. Her idea soon caught on and now many people wear a poppy on Remembrance Day in honour of all those who lost their lives.